Group Dynamics

Icebreakers, Team-Building and Leadership Exercises

Chris Eksteen

Published by Panza Publishers
Panzabyte (PTY) LTD
Reg. No. 2009/020295/07
Koppiesvlei 518, Theunissen, 9410
Free State, South Africa

Copyright of text © 2016 by Chris Eksteen
Copyright of cover image © 2016 by Lizelle Eksteen
Copyright of designs and graphics © 2016 Koppiesvlei Outdoor Education Centre

All rights reserved.

No part of this publication may be reproduced, distributed, or transmitted in any form or by any means, or stored in a database or retrieval system without the prior written permission of the author.

Edited by Suzanne Opperman-Kemp
Proofread by Leon Sebastian Swart, Natáscha Strauss
Cover by Lizelle Eksteen

Printed and bound by Mega Digital in South Africa and CreateSpace in the United States of America, United Kingdom, France, Italy, Japan, New Zealand, Australia, et cetera.

First edition, first print 2016

First edition, Second print 2019

ISBN: 978-0-9946935-5-6 (softcover)
ISBN: 978-0-9946935-6-3 (epub)
ISBN: 978-0-9946935-7-0 (pdf)

PANZA
PUBLISHERS

This book is dedicated to my wife, Delana Eksteen.

Thank you for your love and support.

Experience is the teacher of all things.
JULIUS CAESAR

Contents

Preface	1
Icebreakers	3
Games for Getting to Know One Another	9
Team-building Activities	13
Trust-building Activities	55
Leadership Exercises	61

Preface

In this third book of the *Outdoor Education Resource Series,* I have put together a set of activities that will help improve group dynamics. Most of the activities in this book are well known in the industry, but I have included the versions that have worked best for me in practice. Likewise, once you understand the concept and goal of each activity, you can adjust it to suit your group's needs and environment best.

I hope that you will have fun with your group and discover many wonderful opportunities to teach through play.

I would like to extend a word of thanks to Suzanne Opperman-Kemp for the energy and care you put into this series. Thank you for yet another perfectly edited book.

Thank you to my sister, Lizelle Eksteen, for producing the cover page. Your art and talent is an inspiration. Thank you for all the love and support.

Regards
Chris Eksteen
2016

A Note on Icebreakers

Icebreakers are used to ease the tension within a group of people. Generally, people dislike icebreaker activities, as it takes them out of their comfort zone and forces them to interact with people they don't know. Icebreakers, however, can help strangers feel more comfortable in one another's company and can serve as great conversation starters.

When selecting an icebreaker, take your group's size and average age into consideration. More importantly, make sure your group has fun.

Knights, Horses and Cavaliers

You will need:
- No equipment required.

Site:
- Any open outdoor or indoor space.

How it works:
- Have the group members pair up.
- The partners split off to opposite sides of the playing area.
- One side forms a circle, with their partners standing behind them and forming a bigger outer circle.
- The inner circle rotates clockwise, and the outer circle rotates counterclockwise.
- Yell out either "knights", "horses", or "cavaliers".
- When one of these positions is called out, the group members have to scramble to find their partners and assume the said position (see "Actions").
- The last pair to do so is out of the game, and so it goes until there is a winning team.
- It's fun to make the group members jump and spin or sing while they are rotating in their circles to make it harder for them to keep track of their partners.
- You can also say two or three characters they should do in sequence.

Actions:
- Knights: One partner gets down on one knee and the other partner sits on the kneeling partner's exposed knee with their hands in the air.
- Horses: One partner gets down on all fours and the other partner sits on the kneeling partner's back.
- Cavaliers: One partner picks the other partner up in the style of a groom carrying the bride.

After the session:
- Make sure that the playing area is left behind clean.

Rock, Paper, Scissors

You will need:
- No equipment required.

Site:
- Any space.

How it works:
- Use this game to decide who gets the first turn in an activity, or use it as a time filler.
- Have the group members pair up.
- Count to three. On each count, the pair must wave their fists in a downward motion at each other.
- On the fourth count, they have to show what they have chosen: rock, paper or scissors.
- Rock wins scissors because it can crush it.
- Scissors wins paper because it can cut it.
- Paper wins rock because it can cover it.

Special rules:
- Players are not allowed to change their decision once they've seen what their opponent has chosen.
- They have to show their choice on the fourth count without hesitation.

After the session:
- Make sure that the playing area is left behind clean.

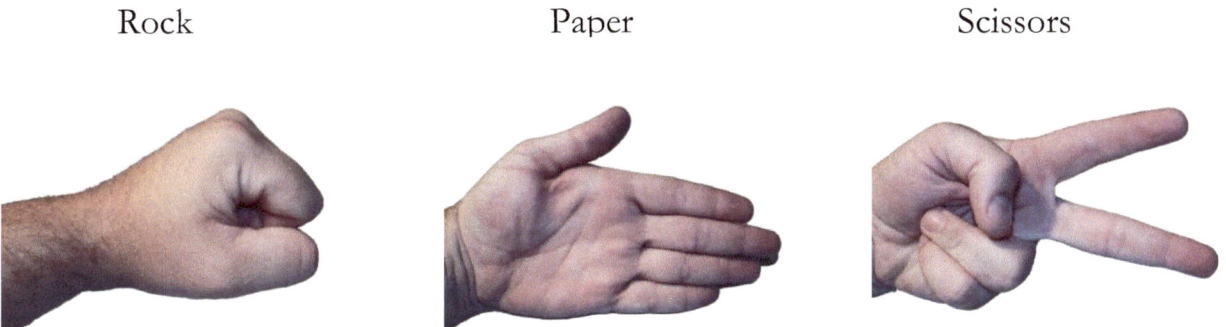

Rock Paper Scissors

Rabbit, Carrot, Gun (Variation on Rock, Paper, Scissors)

You will need:
- No equipment required.

Site:
- Any space.

How it works:
- This game is a variation on rock, paper, scissors. Instead of rock, paper or scissors, players choose rabbit, carrot or gun.
- Rabbit wins carrot because the rabbit eats the carrot.
- Carrot wins gun because the carrot gets stuck in the barrel of the gun.
- Gun wins rabbit because the gun shoots the rabbit.

Special rules:
- See special rules for rock, paper, scissors.

After the session:
- Make sure that the playing area is left behind clean.

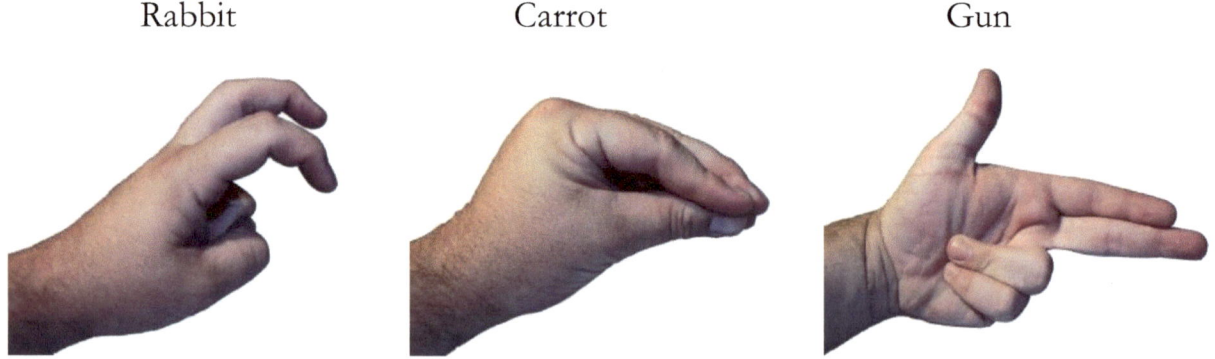

Rabbit   Carrot   Gun

Evolution/Transformation Game (Variation on Rock, Paper, Scissors)

You will need:
- No equipment required.

Site:
- Any space.

How it works:
- Let the whole group stand together.
- Explain to them that they all start as eggs and throughout the game will transform as follows:
  egg → chicken → raptor → dinosaur → fairy → ultimate being (winner)
- Every time a group member meets up with someone who is the same animal as them, they can play a game of rock, paper, scissors. The winner of each round transforms into the next animal in the above sequence, while the loser goes back to being an egg.
- The first person to transform into an ultimate being wins the game.

Actions:
- Egg: Squat down and wobble from side to side as you walk, shouting, "Wobble, wobble, wobble!"
- Chicken: Place your hands in your armpits. Flap your arms like chicken wings and make chicken noises while walking with your back arched.
- Raptor: Point one hand out in front of you, making a snout, and point your other hand behind you, making a tail. Walk while making a high-pitched noise.
- Dinosaur: Stretch out your arms and walk around growling at people.
- Fairy: Flap your arms as if they were wings, singing, "I am a fairy."
- Ultimate being: The final transformation and the winners.

Special rules:
- An egg can only play with an egg, a chicken with a chicken, etc.
- Once you lose a round of rock, paper, scissors, you go back to being an egg, no matter at which stage of transformation you are.

After the session:
- Make sure that the playing area is left behind clean.

Giants, Dwarfs, Wizards (Variation on Rock, Paper, Scissors)

You will need:
- 4 orange cones
- 1 whistle

Site:
- Any large outdoor or indoor space.

How it works:
- This is a large game of rock, paper, scissors.
- Place two orange cones at both ends of the playing field to mark each team's safe zone.
- Divide the group into two teams and let each team stand in their safe zone behind the orange cones.
- Each team has 20 seconds to decide which of the three characters they would like to be.
- On the first whistle, the two teams each form a row in the middle of the playing area. The two teams should be about 3 m apart, facing each other.
- On the second whistle, each team performs their action (see "Actions"), and the winners have to chase the losers back to their safe zone.
- If a team member tags anyone from the opposition, the tagged person must join that team (alternatively, you can reward points per tag).
- To speed things up in the event of a tie (if both teams have chosen the same character), each team can decide the sequence in which they will perform the three actions. That way, if there is a tie, each team can move on to the next action.

Actions:
- Giant: Put your hands above your head and roar.
- Wizard: Put one leg in front of the other, lift your hand and wiggle your fingers. Make a "zzz" sound as your "magic beams" shoot out of your fingers.
- Dwarfs: Squat down, hold up two fingers next to your head like horns and make squeaky mouse sounds.
- Giants win dwarfs because they step on the dwarfs.
- Wizards win giants because they strike the giants with their magic beams.
- Dwarfs win wizards because the magic beams go over the dwarfs' heads.

After the session:
- Put away the orange cones.
- Make sure the playing area is left behind clean.

GET TO KNOW ONE ANOTHER GAMES

These activities are great for getting group members better acquainted with one another.

Toffee Chewer

This activity is only for small groups.

You will need:
- 5 toffees per person (make a note of how many toffees are handed out in total)
- Toilet paper
- A bucket for participants who get nauseous

Site:
- Any space.

How it works:
- Give each person five toffees.
- Take turns and let each person tell the rest of the group five things about themselves, one thing at a time.
- Before each fact about themselves, the person must put a toffee in their mouth.

Special rules:
- Group members can say anything about themselves.
- Group members do not have to eat the toffees if they don't want to.
- Group members are not allowed to eat toffees in between talking about themselves.

After the session:
- Collect all the uneaten toffees.
- Collect all the toffee wrappers.

Face Paint

You will need:
- Enough face paint per team (refill the paint containers when necessary)
- 2 paintbrushes per team
- 1 blindfold per team
- 1 mirror per team
- 1 tin of water per team for the brushes to be washed in.

Site:
- Outdoor area.

How it works:
- Divide the group members into teams of two and give each team their equipment.
- Explain to the group members that this is a trust and communication activity.
- Blindfold one member of each team and let them paint their partner's face.
- Give a set amount of time for the blindfolded person to paint their partner's face.
- When the command is given, the blindfolds must be removed.
- Now the team member whose face has already been painted must put on the blindfold and paint their partner's face. They must attempt to paint their partner's face exactly as their own face has been painted, following the instructions from their partner.
- The team member being painted can hold the paint containers and tell the blindfolded team member how much paint is on the brush, but may not touch the blindfolded team member at all.
- After both team members' faces have been painted, they may look in a mirror.
- The goal is for the team members' faces to be as similar as possible, to show the group how important communication is and how people interpret things differently.

After the session:
- Ask the group to clean their brushes.
- Close the paint containers firmly and clean them if required.
- All group members must wash their hands.
- All the blindfolds and brushes must be collected.

For younger children:

- Guides can paint the children's faces, allowing them to choose the pattern.
- Possible patterns include war stripes, butterflies, dogs, cats, etc.

True or False

You will need:
- No equipment required.

Site:
- Any space.

How it works:
- Ask the group to seat themselves in a circle.
- Each group member gets a turn to tell the rest of the group three things about themselves.
- Two of the three things must be true and one must be false.
- The rest of the group must decide which two things are true and which one is false.
- Guides are welcome to participate in this activity.

After the session:
- Reflection is very important in this activity.
- Explain that this activity breaks the tension and makes everyone feel more comfortable around one another, by taking them out of their comfort zone.
- Ask the group members what new things they have learnt about the rest of the group.

TEAM BUILDING ACTIVITIES

Numbered Chairs

You will need:
- 1 laminated number card per person
- Chairs (see "How it works")

Site:
- Anywhere spacious enough to arrange chairs.

How it works:
- Due to the format of this game, it only works with a certain number of participants. This is because each row needs to have the same number of chairs, and one of the chairs must be empty at all times (see illustration).
- If you have one person too many, you can let that person direct the others. Swap the directing person from time to time with someone else in the group.
- Assign a chair to each group member.
- Arrange the chairs in a block (see illustration) and let a group member sit on each chair, but leave one chair open, e.g.:

  8 people = 3 chairs per row x 3 rows

  11 people = 4 chairs per row x 3 rows, or 3 chairs per row x 4 rows

  15 people = 4 chairs per row x 4 rows
- Put the number cards in a hat and let each person pull one out.
- Group members must now arrange themselves in the chairs in order of their numbers (see "Special Rules"):

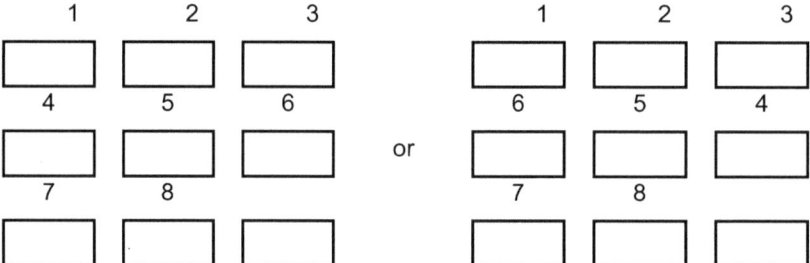

- Once the group has started following a specific pattern (see the two options in the illustration) they have to stick with it in all the rows.
- Only one person may move at a time.

Special rules:
- The group members are not allowed to talk while arranging themselves in sequence.
- Group members may only move forward, backwards or to the side, not diagonally. They may not swap chairs either but must make use of the empty chair.

After the session:
- Let the group members put away their chairs.

Decision-making

You will need:
- 1 activity sheet per group
  - You will find the activity sheet on the page following these instructions.
  - Make a copy for each team and laminate it so that it can be reused, saving time and paper.
- A4 scrap paper for each group
- Pencils for each group

Site:
- Any area where the groups can sit comfortably.

How it works:
- Your group has just received an email. As the president's special committee on home affairs, you need to advise on the following situation:

Urgent message:
Due to an atomic attack that might end the world as we know it, a group of people needs to be taken into a shelter for six months. After the six months, the group of people will be responsible for repopulating the world and rebuilding society. Unfortunately, there are only enough provisions for the remote operation team plus six people. Below is a list of people who are available for selection. Please consult with your team members and advise us on whom to take to the shelter and why. Also, tell us why the others should stay behind.

Of these 12 people, only six can survive:

1. An expectant teacher
2. The teacher's husband – vocation unknown
3. A history professor
4. A cabaret dancer
5. A microbiologist
6. A reverend
7. A policeman with his gun
8. A chartered accountant
9. A president
10. A university student
11. A lawyer
12. A doctor

- Give each group a laminated sheet, some scrap paper and a pencil.
- Give them a brief explanation of what is expected.
- Tell them to read the email carefully before answering.

- If necessary, briefly explain what each of the above 12 vocations entails, e.g. a microbiologist studies microscopic entities such as viruses.
- Give the groups 20 minutes to decide which six people they would save and to write down their reasons.

Discussion:
- Let each group explain their choices to the other groups.
- After the activity, ask how many females are on the list. Answer: 2 (teacher and possibly cabaret dancer).
- Ask how many males are on the list. Answer: 2 (husband and policeman).
- The rest can be either male or female.
- Discuss the pros and cons of each person (see possible answers).
- Tell the group that, although this is not a real-life situation, they have to know that every decision has a consequence.

Possible pros and cons of each person:

1. Expectant teacher
    - + She has a child on the way and starting a new generation will be important.
    - − A baby will take up extra space.

2. The teacher's husband – vocation unknown
    - + The baby will need a father.
    - − We don't know what the husband does for a living. He could be a serial killer.

3. History professor
    - + He/she is clever and could help us learn from history's mistakes.
    - − He/she might be old and not have many years left.

4. Cabaret dancer
    - + She could provide entertainment.
    - − There might be other candidates whose vocations are of more value to society (not that she is not valuable).

5. Microbiologist
    - + He/she can study viruses and other illnesses and can assist the doctor.
    - − Where will he/she find the equipment necessary to do his/her job?

6. Reverend
    - + He/she could help with counselling and spiritual support.
    - − He/she might only cater for a certain religion.

7. Policeman and his gun
   - \+ He could protect the other people.
   - \- He could kill people.

8. Chartered accountant
   - \+ He/she is clever.
   - \- Will we need money in the future?

9. President
   - \+ He/she could have great leadership and problem-solving skills.
   - \- It could be the president of the local tennis club – the email doesn't specify.

10. University student
    - \+ He/she could be a spouse for the teacher's baby and provide a new generation.
    - \- He/she might be young and inexperienced.

11. Lawyer
    - \+ He/she could help settle arguments.
    - \- What if there are no laws in the future?

12. Doctor
    - \+ He/she could cure illnesses and deliver the baby.
    - \- His/her medical knowledge may become outdated in the future.

After the session:
- Collect all the pencils, scrap paper and activity sheets from the group.
- Put the scrap paper in a recycling bin, if available.
- Put away the activity sheets and pencils.

Printable Activity Sheet

Tip: To save paper and time, copy this activity sheet and laminate it so that it can be reused.

Decision-making

Your group has just received an email. As the president's special committee on home affairs, you need to advise on the following situation:

Urgent message:
Due to an atomic attack that might end the world as we know it, a group of people needs to be taken into a shelter for six months. After the six months, the group of people will be responsible for repopulating the world and rebuilding society. Unfortunately, there are only enough provisions for the remote operation team plus six people. Below is a list of people who are available for selection. Please consult with your team members and advise us on whom to take to the shelter and why. Also, tell us why the others should stay behind.

Of these 12 people, only six can survive

1. An expectant teacher
2. The teacher's husband – vocation unknown
3. A history professor
4. A cabaret dancer
5. A microbiologist
6. A reverend
7. A policeman with his gun
8. A chartered accountant
9. A president
10. A university student
11. A lawyer
12. A doctor

What are your choices and why?
_____
_____
_____
_____
_____
_____
_____
_____
_____

Communication Conundrum

You will need:
- 1 set of 13 cards that spell out COMMUNICATION per team
  - Type out the letters of COMMUNICATION on a single sheet of paper, print one copy for each group, cut out the letters and laminate them.

C	O	M	M
U	N	I	C
A	T	I	O
N			

Site:
- Any space where a table is available.

How it works:
- Ask each group to use all their cards to form one word. The correct answer is COMMUNICATION.
- Variation: Each group must spell as many words as they can with the 13 letters and try to find the longest one. (They can use the letter M as a W and the letter N as a Z.) Here are some examples:

A

- account
- act
- action
- aim
- am
- ammo
- ammunition
- amount
- an
- anoint
- anomic
- ant
- anti
- antic
- at
- ATM
- atom
- atomic
- auction
- aunt
- auto

C

- Cain
- cam
- can
- cannot
- canon
- cat
- caution
- coat
- coco
- cocoa
- coconut
- coin
- comic
- commit
- common
- contain
- coo
- cot
- count
- cow
- cut

I

- Ian
- icon
- in
- inn
- into
- ion
- ionic
- it

M

- main
- man
- mat
- mimic
- mini
- minicam
- mint
- moan
- mom
- Mona
- moo
- moon
- mot
- motion
- mount
- mountain
- mow
- mum

N

- nation
- Nico
- nit
- no
- non
- noon
- not
- notion
- noun
- now
- nun
- nut

O

- onion
- out
- own

T

- tan
- Tim
- tin
- to
- Tom
- tonic
- too
- tow
- town
- tuna
- twin
- two

U

- uncommon
- union
- unit
- Uno
- unto

W

- wait
- want
- win
- wit
- woman
- won
- wow

Z

- zinc
- zoo
- zoom

A good resource to use:
- www.wordhippo.com

After the session:
- Fasten each set of cards with a rubber band and put it away.

Paper Plate Auction

You will need:
- A stack of paper plates with various money values, ranging from high to low, written on them
- Play money for each team, made from scrap paper – larger notes for larger amounts and smaller notes for smaller amounts
    - You could also print out the play money and laminate it.
- Extra play money for the auction bank so that change can be given on bids

Site:
- Any space where the wind will not blow the play money away.

How it works:
- Ask the teams if they know what an auction is. If necessary, explain how an auction works (the highest bidder gets the item on auction).
- Assign someone the role of auctioneer.
- Supply each team with play money to the value of about 3 000.
- Tell the teams what the values of the plates are, but do not reveal which plate has which value.
- The teams must now bid against each other for the paper plates.
- The auctioneer will accept the highest bid for each plate.
- The winning team must pay for the plate with their play money before the value of the plate is revealed and handed to them.
- Teams may use the paper plates they have won to pay for new plates.
- Plates that have been used to pay with can be auctioned off again.
- At the end of the game, the team with the most money (including the values of their plates) is the winning team.

Discussion:
- Explain to the group that each action and decision has a consequence.

After the session:
- Collect all the money and plates from the teams and put it away.

Printable Activity Sheet

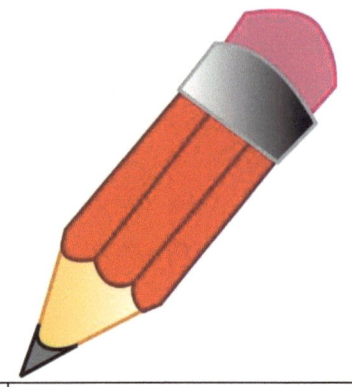

Play money 1	Play money 2	Play money 5
Play money 10	Play money 20	Play money 50
Play money 100	Play money 200	Play money 500

Puzzle Shapes (Tangrams)

You will need:

- A set of seven tangram puzzle pieces per team
    - Print out one sheet of seven tangram puzzle pieces per group (see image).
    - Carefully cut out the puzzle pieces.
    - Make a dot on the back of each puzzle piece.
    - For a long-term solution, take your tangram sheet to a carpenter and ask them to cut the pieces out of wood. You can then paint a dot on the back of each piece. These wooden pieces will last a long time and save paper.

Site:

- Any space that has an even surface to work on.

How it works:

- Firstly, instruct each group to build a square or triangle with all seven puzzle pieces.
- Once a group has finished building a square or triangle, let them attempt building a more difficult shape (see "Solutions").

Special rules:

- The puzzle pieces may not be broken.
- All seven pieces must be used to build the shape.
- The dotted sides must be at the bottom.

Solutions:

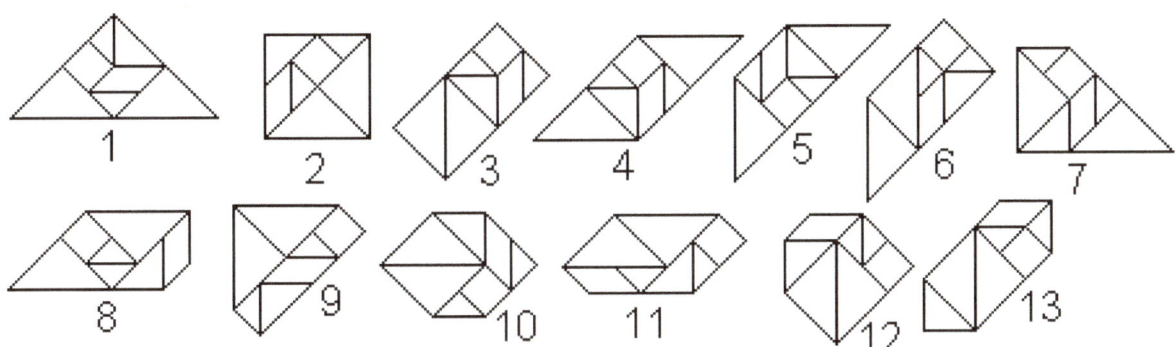

The first four shapes are:

Triangle – Square – Rectangle – Parallelogram

After the session:

- Fasten each set of puzzle pieces with a rubber band and put it away.

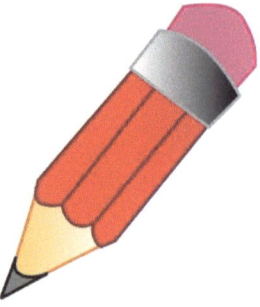 # Printable Activity Sheet

Tip: To save paper and time, copy this activity sheet and laminate it so that it can be reused.

24

Human Shapes

You will need:
- No equipment required.

Site:
- Outdoor or indoor area with plenty of space.

How it works:
- Divide the group into teams of equal numbers.
- Give the teams a shape to build within 30 seconds, using their bodies, sound and motion (see examples).
- The team that has built the most accurate shape wins.
- If you have time left, get the whole group (all the teams) to build a machine. It should have space for at least one passenger and be able to move forward at least 3 m. Give the group unlimited time to do this.

Examples of shapes:
- Bicycle
- Cartoon
- Cell phone
- Chair
- Church
- Cow
- Dog
- Elephant
- Everest
- Fountain
- Giraffe
- Goat
- Hippo
- Jet ski
- Mouse
- Number 47
- Pineapple
- Plane
- Pyramid
- Racecar
- Rock
- Snake
- Speed bike
- Tomato
- Tortoise
- Traffic jam
- Tree
- Waterfall
- Whale
- Windmill

Special rules:
- The shape can be either 3D or flat on the ground (2D).
- All the team members must form part of the shape.

After the session:
- Emphasise how important communication was in completing this activity. Explain to the group that communication also plays an important role in life.
- Highlight how working together is an important part of successfully completing a task.

Giant Pick-up Sticks

You will need:
- 31 coloured sticks (1 black, 2 white, 7 red, 7 green, 7 yellow and 7 blue)
    - Take 31 round wooden dell sticks of 8 mm in diameter and about 40–50 cm in length. Slightly sharpen the one end of each stick, and paint them in the colours specified above.
- 1 laminated scorecard
- 1 wooden dice
    - Paint a small wooden block as playing dice. Remember that opposite sides of the dice should always equal 7. Therefore, 6 and 1 should be opposite each other, as should 3 and 4, and 5 and 2.

Site:
- Any area with ample space.

How it works:
- Divide the group into teams of an equal number.
- The black and white sticks count the most points, so place them down on the ground first.
- Stand the other sticks upright over the black and white sticks, holding them all together vertically in one hand. Let go gently and allow the sticks to drop where they may.
- Let the teams take turns to roll the dice. The team who rolls the highest number gets to go first.
- The first team may now start by picking up any stick.
- While picking up a stick, teams are not allowed to move or stir any of the other sticks. Should this happen, the team member has to place the stick they were removing back on the pile, and then the turn goes to the next team.
- A team may use sticks that they have already won to pick up other sticks one by one.
- If a team makes use of a stick to pick up another one and any of the other sticks move, they will lose all the sticks they have won so far.
- Teams will receive points for every stick they pick up. Points are allocated according to the colour of the sticks:

    Black = 25 points   Blue = 5 points
    White = 15 points   Green = 2 points
    Red = 7 points   Yellow = 1 point

- The team with the highest score at the end of the game wins.
- Ensure that all team members get a chance to play

Special rules:
- Teams may only pick up one stick per turn.

After the session:
- Collect all the sticks and put them away, along with the dice and scorecard.

Helium Stick

You will need:

- 1 x 4 m push-in tent pole
    - You can buy one from any outdoor store, or use one from an old tent.
    - The tent pole should be light and preferably have an elastic cord in the middle.
    - You will use this tent pole as your "helium stick".

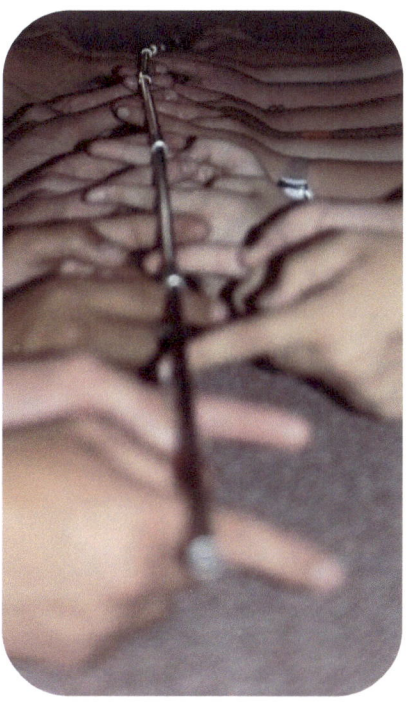

Site: Anywhere spacious enough.

How it works:

- The aim is to lower the helium stick to the ground by means of teamwork.
- Line your group up, either in a single line or in two lines facing each other.
- Ask the group to put their index fingers out straight in front of them at shoulder height.
- Explain that you are now going to place a helium-filled stick on their fingers and that they must lower it to the ground.
- NOTE: In reality, there is no helium in the stick, but don't tell the group. The secret is that the collective upwards pressure of everyone's fingers trying to touch the stick is greater than the weight of the stick. Therefore, the stick seems to "float" upwards.
- Now place the stick on the group's fingers, but keep hold of it until you give the instruction for it to be lowered.
- Tell them that everyone's index finger should touch the stick and that they can only start lowering it when you give the instruction.

- As soon as the group starts lowering the stick, it will start "floating" over their heads.
- Now take the stick from them.
- Suggest that the group discuss their strategy and try again.
- Line them up once more and let them try again. The stick will "float" up every time.

Rules:

- The group members are not allowed to grab the stick.
- At all times, their fingers should be straight and in contact with the bottom of the stick.

After the session:

- Disassemble the tent pole and put it away.

Helium Hoop (Variation on Helium Stick)

You will need:
- 1 hula hoop

Site:
- Any suitable area.

How it works:
- See the instructions and rules for the helium stick activity, but replace the tent pole with the hula hoop.
- Instead of forming a line, let the group form a circle around the hula hoop.

After the session:
- Put the hula hoop away.

Wonky Tower (Tabletop or Giant)

You will need:

- Tabletop version: 1 wonky tower set, e.g. Jenga
    - You could also make your own blocks. Take a 1 x 1 cm wooden plank and cut 60 blocks, each of which is 4 cm long.
    - Optionally, you can paint the blocks.
    - Use an old tub or canvas bag to store your home-made building blocks.
- Giant version: 1 giant wonky tower set, e.g. Jenga Giant
    - You could also make your own blocks. Take a 5 x 5 cm wooden plank and cut 60 blocks, each of which is 25 cm long.
    - Optionally, you can paint the blocks.
    - Use an old tub or canvas bag to store your home-made building blocks.

Site:

- Indoor or outdoor area with a flat and even surface.

How it works:

- Build a tower with the blocks, stacking rows of three blocks each. Every second row should face in the opposite direction as the preceding row (see image).
- As soon as the tower is finished the game can begin.
- The teams can now take turns to remove a block from the tower and place it on top, in keeping with the tower's pattern. They should do this without making the tower fall over.
- Once the block has been placed on top of the tower, it is the other team's turn.
- The team that causes the tower to fall over loses the game and has to rebuild the stack for another round.

Special rules:

- Teams may not remove a block from the top three layers.
- Once a team member has started pulling on a block, they are not allowed to return it; they have to take that block out.
- There is an additional rule for the tabletop version: A team member may only use one hand at a time to remove a block.

After the session:

- Pack all the blocks away neatly in their tub or bag.

Gutter Game

You will need:
- 20 pieces of gutter (30 cm each) per team
- 1 gutter bend per team
- 1 gutter hole fitment per team
- 2 gutter blockers per team
    - The gutter pieces, bend, hole fitment and blockers can be bought from any hardware store.
- 1 tennis or ping pong ball per team
- 4 orange cones or beacons

Site:
- Outdoor area with enough space.

How it works:
- Divide each team's gutter pieces, including the bend, hole fitment and blockers, among the team members.
- Mark the start and finish point with the cones. These two points should be a few metres apart.
- Each team must now work together to get their ball from the start to finish point.
- The ball is not allowed to touch the ground.
- All gutter pieces, including the bend, hole fitment and blockers, MUST be used.
- No one is allowed to touch the ball.
- You can also put obstacles in the teams' way, e.g. stumps they need to climb over.
- The first team to get their ball to the finish point is the winning team.

Special rules:
- Every person must carry the ball at least once.
- If the ball falls, the group has to go back to the start point.
- Team members may not move while the ball is in their gutter piece. They must wait for another team member to fetch it from them.

After the session:
- Wash and dry all equipment used.
- Put all the equipment away.

Gutter Game (Water Variation)

You will need:

- 20 pieces of gutter (30 cm each) per team
- 1 gutter bend per team
- 1 gutter hole fitment per team
- 2 gutter blockers per team
    - The gutter pieces, bend, hole fitment and blockers can be bought from any hardware store.
- 1 bucket filled with water per team
- 1 empty bucket per team
- 1 l tub per team (use it to fill the pipe)
- 4 orange cones or beacons

Site:

- Outdoor area with enough space.

How it works:

- See instructions for the original gutter game.
  Instead of transferring a ball, teams will transfer the water in the bucket at the start point to the empty bucket at the finish point using the 1 l tub.
- The team that transfers the most water to the bucket at the finish point is the winning team.

Special rules:

- If a team spills water, they have to go back to the start point.
- All of the gutter pieces must be used.
- Team members may not move while the water is in their gutter piece. They must wait for another team member to fetch it from them.

After the session:

- Pour all the water out of the buckets – preferably into the garden.
- Dry all the buckets and put them away.
- Wash and dry all other equipment used.
- Put all the equipment away.

Good Day, Scott

You will need:
- No equipment required.

Site:
- Any area in which the group can sit in a spacious circle.

How it works:
- Let the group form a big circle, sitting not too far from one another.
- Everyone in the circle is now called Scott.
- The sequence is as follows:
    - One person starts by greeting the person next to them with the words, "Good day, Scott."
    - The second person then replies, "Good day, Scott."
    - The first person then says to the second person, "Say good day to Scott, Scott."
    - The second person then turns to the person on their other side and says, "Good day, Scott."
    - That third person replies, "Good day, Scott."
    - The second person then says to the third person, "Say good day to Scott, Scott."
- The game continues in this sequence around the circle.
- Once a person makes a mistake, their name changes from Scott to Kevin.
- When that person makes a second mistake, their name changes from Kevin to Trevor.
- When a third mistake is made, their name changes from Trevor to Liam.
- After making a fourth mistake, the person falls out and must leave the circle, while the others continue with the game.

After the session:
- Explain to the group how important it is to pay attention, otherwise, you can make mistakes.

Good Day, Scott (Female Version)

How it works:
- See the instructions for the original version.
- For all-female groups, replace the male names with the following female names:
    - Scott – Charlotte
    - Kevin – Kate
    - Trevor – Tracy
    - Liam – Lindy
- You can stick with the male version for smaller children of either sex.
- For co-ed schools, you can run both versions simultaneously.
- Make sure you keep track of the names.

Blind Dodgeball

You will need:
- 1 orange cone or beacon per team
- 1 blindfold per team
- 1 plastic ball or tennis ball per team (the colour of the ball must be different for each team)
- 1 rope per team (tied in a circle)
- 1 whistle

Site:
- An outdoor area that is free of any hazards and where blindfolded people won't hurt themselves.

How it works:
- Each team has to nominate a player to be blindfolded.
- Each team has to nominate a director.
- Show each team which cone, rope circle and ball is theirs.
- The team members who are not blindfolded must stay behind the cone and inside the rope circle.
- The first round starts with one blow of the whistle.
- Each blindfolded player must now find their team's ball and try to hit the other teams' blindfolded players with it while dodging the other teams' balls. They must do this by following the instructions from their team's director.
- Once a blindfolded player has been hit by another team's ball, they have to go sit down by their team's cone.

- If a blindfolded player picks up another team's ball and throws it at another player, they are disqualified and must go sit down by their team's cone.
- Once a player has been eliminated, the team must choose a new player to be blindfolded.
- Once all but one team has been completely eliminated, blow the whistle twice to indicate the end of the round.
- Give the eliminated teams time to blindfold new players.
- The blindfolded player of the team that has not been eliminated will play again in the next round.
- Blow the whistle once to indicate the start of the next round.
- The team that wins the most rounds wins the game.

Special rules:
- If a team member steps outside their team's rope circle, they are disqualified.
- No one may touch the blindfolded person.

After the session:
- Explain how important communication is.
- Give tips on how the teams can improve their communication.
- Wash and dry the blindfolds, and put them away with the rest of the equipment.

Holey Pipes

You will need:

- 2 pipes with holes per team
    - Use a 1 m piece of PVC pipe (drain piping of 110 mm in width works well). Glue an end cap on the one side. Drill 4 mm holes all around the pipe at different heights.
- 2 x 1 l buckets per team
- 2 ping pong balls per team
- 1 whistle

Site:

- Any area with a pool, dam or another source of water close by.

How it works:

- Position each team's pipe vertically, about 5–10 m away from the water source, depending on the age of the participants.
- Put a ping pong ball inside every pipe.
- Let each team nominate a runner.
- Blow the whistle to start the game.
- The runner of each team must fetch water with the bucket and run back to pour it into their team's pipe.
- The rest of the team must try to plug the holes in the pipe with their fingers in order to prevent water from spilling out.
- The first team whose ping pong ball pops out at the top of the pipe is the winning team.

Special rules:

- Team members are not allowed to remove the ping pong ball from the pipe with their hands; it has to pop out freely.
- Teams may not move the pipe closer to the water.

After the session:

- Rinse all the equipment and allow it to dry in the sun.
- Put all the equipment away.

Mutant Polar Bear

You will need:
- No equipment required.

Site:
- Large outdoor area (about 100 m long).

How it works:
- Let the group form a line next to one another.
- Tell the group that a mutant polar bear named Fred is chasing them. (If necessary, explain what "mutant" means and what a polar bear is.)
- Instruct the group to take only one deep breath and run away from Fred as fast as they can, while screaming as loud as they can, until they run out of breath.
- Group members must run one by one when instructed.
- As soon as a group member is out of breath or stops screaming, they have to stop where they are.
- The group member who manages to run the furthest in just one breath is the winner.

Special rules:
- Group members are not allowed to keep running after they have stopped screaming.
- Each group member may only take one deep breath. When they are out of breath, they must stop running.

After the session:
- Let the group members rest and have some water.

Screaming Toes

You will need:
- 1 whistle
- 1 water pistol per person (optional)

Site:
- Any area big enough for the group to sit comfortably.

How it works:
- Let the group sit in a circle with their legs straight out in front of them. All group members must look at their toes.
- Once the whistle blows, everyone can look up at anyone else in the circle.
- Once two group members look each other straight in the eyes, both must start screaming as loudly as they can.
- Alternatively, give each group member a water pistol. When two group members catch each other's eye, they must squirt each other with water instead of screaming.
- There are no winners in this game – it is just for fun.

Special rules:
- Group members must look down at their toes until the whistle blows.
- When the whistle blows, group members may not look around; they may only look at one person.
- Group members are only allowed to scream when looking directly at someone who is looking directly at them.
- When using water pistols, group members are not allowed to shoot each other in the face.

After the session:
- If water pistols were used, dry them off properly and put them away.

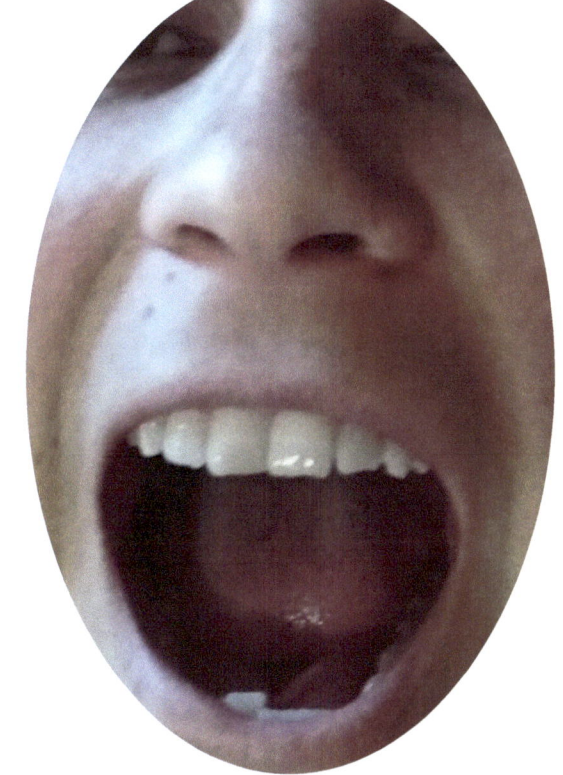

Mafia

You will need:
- 6 pieces of folded paper with the following written inside:
    - Mafia (3 pieces of paper)
    - Police (2 pieces of paper)
    - Doctor (1 piece of paper)
- 1 blank piece of folded paper for each of the remaining group members
- A container for group members to pull the pieces of paper out of

Site:
- Indoor areas work best.

How it works:
- The object of the game is for the police to find the mafia before all the citizens or the police themselves are killed by the mafia.
- Have the group sit in a circle.
- Each group member must draw a piece of paper from the container.
- Three group members will be mafia members, two will be police officers and one will be the doctor.
- The rest of the group members, who drew blank pieces of paper, will be normal citizens.
- The group members may not know one another's identities.
- Once everyone knows their own identity, collect all the pieces of paper from the group.
- Everyone must now close their eyes and look down.
- First round:
    - The guide tells the doctor to wake up.→Only the doctor opens their eyes.
    - The guide tells the doctor to go back to sleep.→The doctor closes their eyes again.
    - The guide tells the police to wake up.→Only the two police officers open their eyes and see each other.
    - The guide tells the police to go to sleep.→The police officers close their eyes again.
    - The guide tells the mafia to wake up.→Only the three mafia members open their eyes and see one another.
    - The guide now knows who is who.
    - While awake, the mafia has to silently agree on and point at someone they want to kill.
    - The guide tells the mafia to go to sleep.→The mafia members close their eyes again.
    - The guide tells the doctor to wake up.→The doctor points at a person they want to save.
    - The guide tells the doctor to go to sleep.→The doctor closes their eyes again.
    - The guide tells the police to wake up.→The police officers open their eyes.
    - The guide asks the police who they think the mafia members are.
    - The police officers then silently have to agree upon and point at one person they think is part of the mafia.
    - The guide tells the police to go to sleep.→The police officers close their eyes.
    - The guide tells everyone to wake up.→Everyone opens their eyes.

- - The guide now tells everyone who was killed by the mafia and who was saved by the doctor.
  - If the doctor saved the person who was killed, that person can keep playing. If not, the murdered person is out of the game and must go and sit in the middle of the circle.
  - The guide then tells the group which person the police officers have accused of being in the mafia.
  - The accused person then has to defend themselves in "court" and explain why they can't be a mafia member. All the citizens then take a vote as to whether the accused is guilty or not.
  - If the village finds the accused guilty, the accused is sentenced to jail and must also go and sit in the middle of the circle.
  - Once the accused has been found guilty, they must reveal their identity (doctor, police, mafia or citizen).
  - If the accused is found not guilty, they stay in the game and their identity remains a secret.
- Following rounds: Repeat the above steps.
- The game ends once all the police officers are dead, once all the citizens are dead, or once all the mafia members have been caught.
- When the game is over, everyone can reveal their identities.

Special rules:
- If the doctor gets killed, the game continues without a doctor.

After the session:
- Make sure the area is left clean.
- Put all the pieces of paper in a recycling bin, if available.

Walking Planks

You will need:

- 1 pair of walking planks per team
    - Take two long planks (each about 2 m long) and drill holes into them about 40 cm apart.
    - Feed a piece of rope (1 m long) through each hole and tie a knot at the bottom so the rope cannot pass through the hole. This rope will become a handle for team members to hold onto.
- 4 orange cones or beacons to indicate the start and finish line
- 1 whistle

Site:

- In the parking lot or any other flat surface.

How it works:

- All team members must stand behind the start line with one foot on each plank and a piece of rope in each hand.
- When the whistle blows the teams must move towards the finish line, wearing the planks as "shoes".
- The first team to completely cross the finish line with their planks wins.
- You can also have the teams complete timed laps. The team with the best time wins.

Special rules:

- No team members are allowed to step off the planks.
- If a team member steps off a plank, the whole team has to return to the start line.

After the session:

- Put all the equipment away.

Hula Hoop Pass

You will need:
- 1 hula hoop per team
- 1 whistle

Site:
- Any area with enough space for team members to line up.

How it works:
- Let each team form a row and hold hands.
- Give the person at the start of each team's line a Hula Hoop.
- The game starts when the whistle blows.
- The team now has to pass the hula hoop from one side of the line to the other without letting go of one another's hands.
- The first team to finish is the winning team.
- If you only have one Hula Hoop, you can have timed laps between the teams. The team with the best time wins.

After the session:
- Put the hula hoops away.

Tennis Ball Chin Pass

You will need:
- 1 tennis ball per team
- 1 whistle

Site:
- Outdoor area with enough space for teams to line up.

How it works:
- Let each of the teams form a line, with the team members standing behind one another.
- Put a ball under the chin of the team member who is first in line.
- The game starts when the whistle blows.
- The team members must now pass the ball down the line using only their chins and necks (no hands).
- The first team whose ball reaches the end of their line wins.
- Depending on the number of people, teams can also be instructed to pass the ball to the end of the line and back in order to win.

Special rules:
- No one is allowed to use their hands to pass the ball.
- The ball is not allowed to fall on the ground. If it does, the team has to start from the beginning.

After the session:
- Put all the equipment away.

Soccer Ball Feet Pass

You will need:
- 1 soccer ball per team
- 1 whistle

Site:
- Outdoor area with enough space for teams to line up.

How it works:
- Let each team lie on their backs next to one another with their feet in the air.
- Balance the ball on the feet of the first person in line.
- The game starts when the whistle blows.
- Each team must now pass the ball from one end of the line to the other, using only their feet.
- The first team whose ball reaches the end of the line wins.
- If you have only one ball, you can have timed laps between the teams. The team with the best time wins.

Special rules:
- No one is allowed to use their hands to pass the ball.
- If the ball touches the ground, the team has to go back to the start.
- If the ball falls but doesn't touch the ground, the next person in line can grab the ball, as long as only their feet and legs are used.

After the session:
- Put all the equipment away.

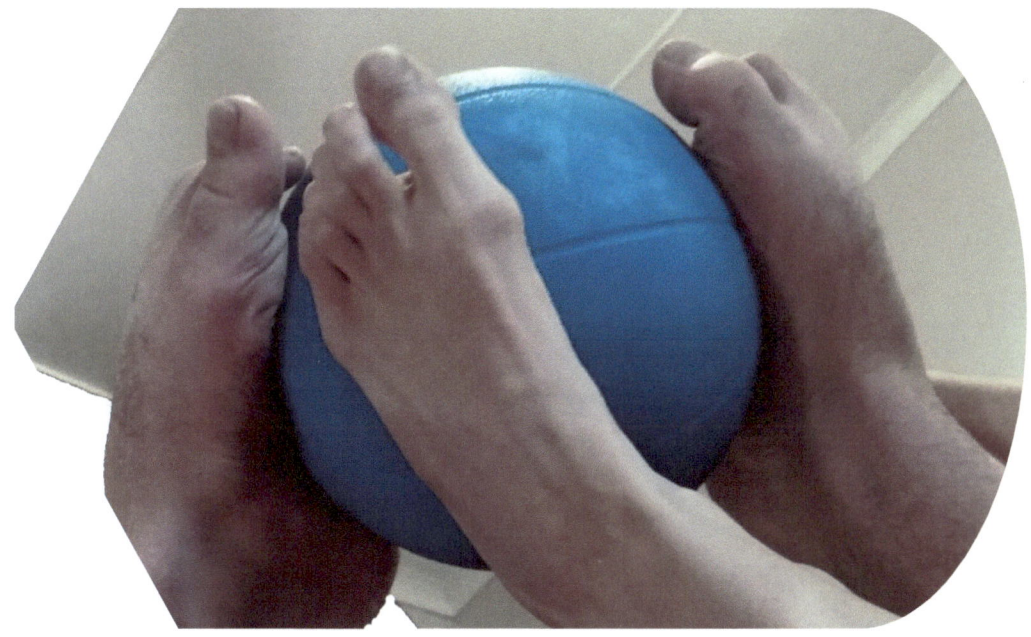

Water Bucket Balance

You will need:
- 1 bucket per team
- Enough water to fill all the buckets
- Stopwatch

Site:
- Outdoor area.

How it works:
- Make sure team members are wearing clothes that can get wet and that their cell phones and other electronic devices are not nearby.
- Let each team form a circle, lying on their backs with their legs up in the air and facing inwards.
- The team's feet must be bottoms up and as flat as possible to form a single platform in the middle of the circle.
- Put a bucket filled with water on each team's feet and count to three before letting go.
- The team that can balance the bucket the longest is the winning team.
- You can also let the team members switch between left and right feet, or between girls and boys holding it.

Special rules:
- Team members may only balance the bucket using their feet.

After the session:
- Let the buckets dry out and put them away.

Giant Dominoes

You will need:
- 1 set of giant dominoes
    - You can also make your own dominoes. Take a wooden plank and cut out rectangles of about 20 cm x 10 cm. Now paint domino dots on them.

Site:
- Any area with a flat surface.

How it works:
- Shuffling the dominoes
    - Before a game begins, the domino tiles need to be shuffled. Turn them all face down and move the tiles around at random so no player can track the position of the tiles. Now put the shuffled tiles in a pile, still face down. This pile is called the boneyard.

- Starting the game
    - In order to determine who goes first, each player must draw a random tile from the boneyard. The player with the highest face value will get to play first, and from there the group may play in either a clockwise or counterclockwise direction. Once the order of play has been established, the dominoes must be returned to the boneyard for shuffling.

- Drawing tiles
    - Each player must draw 7 dominoes from the boneyard.
    - Once the players begin drawing tiles, they must place them face down so that other players cannot see their value. However, the drawn tiles may not be hidden, as players need to see how many dominoes are still in play.

- Placing the first tile
    - Once all the players have drawn their dominoes, the first player places their first tile face up on the playing surface.

- Placing subsequent tiles
    - The subsequent tiles must be added onto the open end of the tiles already in play (in other words, the end of the tile that doesn't have another tile touching it). The only exception to this rule is with doubles, which may be placed sideways to form a "T". This will lead to two open ends for other players to add onto.
    - Dominoes can be placed either in line with the other dominoes or at an angle, creating an "L" turn in the layout's open end.
    - The two adjoining sides of the dominoes in play should always have the same value.
    - If the player does not have a tile with the open end's value, they need to draw another tile from the boneyard, while the turn passes to the next player.

- Some rules state that a player must draw tiles from the boneyard until they draw a tile that can be used in play.
- Once the boneyard is picked dry (or there are no more tiles left to draw), players must skip turns until they can use the tiles they have drawn.

- Ending a game
  - A game ends once a player has played all their tiles. Traditionally, the player must say "domino" when playing their last tile.

After the session:
- Pack all the dominoes back in their box or tub.

This is an example of a domino set.

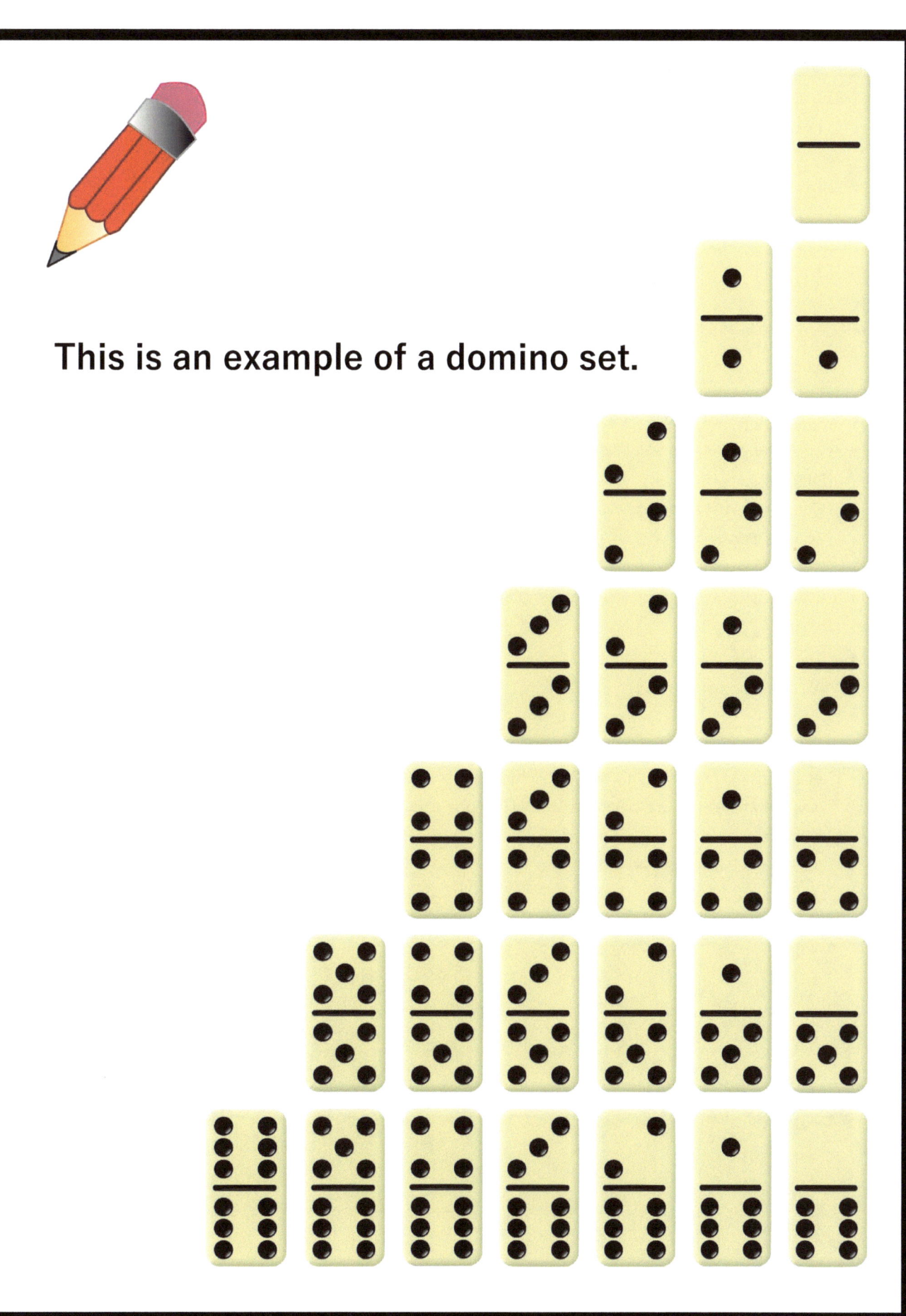

Nail Balancing

You will need:

- 1 wooden block with one long nail hammered into it per team
    - To make the game a bit more difficult, you can hammer in a few shorter nails around the long nail (see images below).
- 10 loose nails per team

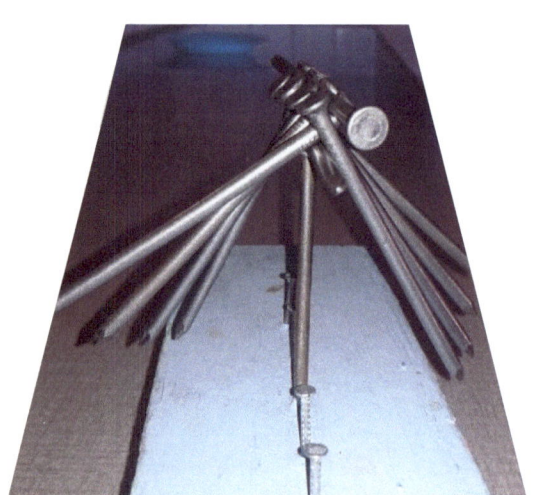

Site:

- Any area with a flat surface.

How it works:

- Place the wooden block on a flat surface.
- Each team must now balance all 10 nails on the one long nail.
- None of the 10 balancing nails may touch the wooden block.
- The first team to achieve this, wins.

Special rules:

- The 10 nails may only balance on the one long nail in the block.
- All 10 nails must be used.

After the session:

- At a Christian camp, explain how we all form part of one body (Eph. 4:16). Pull the one long nail out to show how the whole structure collapses without it. If one part or person is taken out, the rest of the group cannot function.
- Put the equipment away.

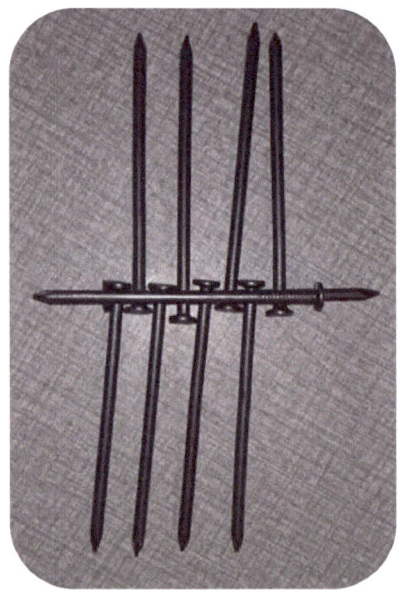

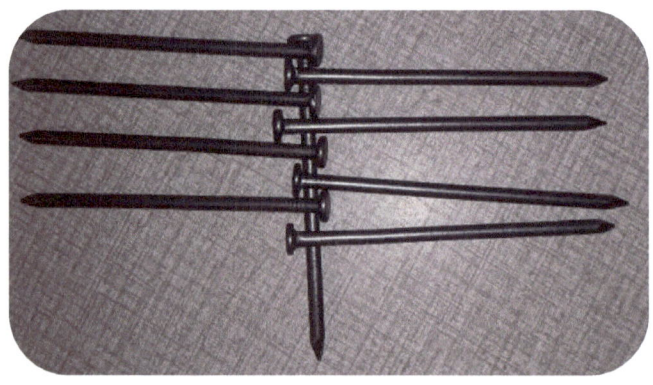

Hacky sack (Footbag)

You will need:

- 1 hacky sack per team

Site:

- Anywhere with a flat surface.

How it works:

- Let each team stand in a circle.
- Any team member can start by passing the hacky sack with their foot to another player.
- The hacky sack needs to be kept in the air for as long as possible while being passed from one player to another.
- When the hacky sack touches the ground, the game restarts.
- If everyone in the circle has touched the hacky sack within a round, it is called a hack. The team gets a point for every hack.
- Every time the hacky sack touches the ground, the team forfeits all the hack points they have scored up to that point and have to start from zero again.
- If a player breaks any of the rules (see below) they have to bow forward and another player will punish them by throwing the hacky at their bum.

Special rules:

- Hands may not be used, unless when punishment is being served.
- Players may not self-serve, but must always pass the hacky sack to someone else.
- No hack abuse is allowed: Players may not step on or kick the hacky sack. If a player misses someone while punishing them, it also counts as abuse.
- No "hack-sterbation": Players may not play the hacky sack more than three times consecutively.
- Players are not allowed to say sorry or make any form of apology in any language.

After the session:

- Put the hacky sacks away.

Murder Wink

You will need:
- No equipment required.

Site:
- Indoor areas work best.

How it works:
- Choose one person in the group to be a police officer.
- The police officer is sent out of the room.
- Once the police officer has left the room, the remaining group will choose a murderer.
- Once the murderer has been chosen, the police officer is called back, unaware of who the murderer is.
- The murderer now has to "kill" off group members by winking at them, without the police officer catching them.
- The police officer has to catch the murderer before the whole group is dead.
- Once the police officer catches the murderer, the game restarts. In the next round, the murderer from the previous game will play the police officer.

After the session:
- Make sure the area is left clean.

When the Wind Blows

You will need:
- 1 chair per person
- 1 spare chair, in case other breaks

Site:
- Large outdoor area in the shade.

How it works:
- Let the whole group sit in a circle on their chairs.
- Make sure there are no hazardous objects that players could hit their heads on, should they fall over.
- The guide stands in the middle of the circle and recites the following rhyme: "When the wind blows, it blows to all of those…" The rhyme can be completed with any description, e.g. "… wearing jeans".
- Now all the players wearing jeans have to jump up and find another chair.
- The guide also runs to find a chair, which means there will be one less chair for the group members.
- The person who was too slow to find a chair now has to stand in the middle and recite the rhyme.
- Once the rhyme has been recited, the person in the middle must run to find a chair, leaving someone else without a chair.
- The game continues in this fashion.

Special rules:
- Players are not allowed to swop chairs with the person next to them.
- If a player fits the description given at the end of the rhyme but does not run to find a chair, they will be sent to the middle.

After the session:
- Players must stack their chairs neatly and put them away.

S-P-U-D

You will need:

- 1 soccer- or basketball

Site:

- Outdoor area.

How it works:

- Let the group form a circle about 2 m wide.
- Every group member receives a secret number. These numbers can either be drawn from a hat or the guide can whisper each person's number in their ear.
- One person is chosen to be "it" and goes to stand in the middle of the circle with the ball.
- The person who is "it" throws the ball up in the air and shouts a number.
- The person whose number has been called must run to catch the ball, while the rest of the group run away.
- As soon as the person whose number has been called catches the ball, they must shout, "Stop!"
- Everyone running away then has to stop in their tracks.
- The person who caught the ball can now give two big steps towards the rest of the group and throw the ball at one person in the group.
- The person being thrown is not allowed to move their feet, but may only dodge the ball by moving the rest of their body.
- If the person gets hit, they get the letter "S" against their name and is now "it".
- Every time a person gets hit, another letter is added to their name. "P" is next, then "U", then "D". As soon as the word "SPUD" is spelt out against a person's name, they are out of the game.
- If the person throwing the ball misses the person they want to hit, they get a letter against their name and stays "it".

After the session:

- Put the soccer ball away.

Animal Kingdom Cards

You will need:

- 1 set of cards
  - You can make and laminate cards to fit the animals in your area or country. Here are a few examples:

Site:
- Indoor or outdoor area.

How it works:
- Divide the cards evenly between the members of the group.
- Each player must hold their packet of cards so that only they can see the information on it.
- One player starts and calls out one of the categories on their top card, along with its statistic, e.g. "Speed: 25 km/h".
- One at a time, each of the other players call out their top card's statistic for the same category (i.e. Speed).
- The player whose top card has the highest value in that category gets the other players' top cards and puts them at the bottom of their pile, together with their own top card.
- If two or more cards have the same value, the player calls out another category to determine a winner from the players with the same value.
- At the start of each round, the winner of the previous round can call out the next category.
- The game ends when one player has won all the cards.
- Only the top card may be used for statistics, until there are only three cards left in a player's hand. Then they may choose between cards to get the highest statistic.

After the session:
- Fasten each set of cards with rubber bands and put it away.

TRUST ACTIVITIES

Trust-building Activities

IMPORTANT: Please follow the order of these activities, as trust is earned and developed step by step:

- Wind in the willows
- Trust lean
- Trust run (Guillotine)
- Trust fall
- Trust walk

Wind in the Willows

You will need:

- No equipment required.

Site:

- Any spacious area.

How it works:

- Divide the group into smaller groups and let them stand in a tight circle, shoulder to shoulder, all in the spotting position (see the instructions for trust lean).

- One person stands in the middle with their feet together and their arms crossed over their chest. They start to fall and the people in the circle need to catch and pass the person around.
- The person in the middle gets 10–20 seconds and then gives the next person a chance.
- Each member of the group should get a turn.
- Make sure that the person in the middle is back on their feet before breaking the circle.

Special rules:

- No one is allowed to push or shove the person in the middle, but may only gently pass them on.
- No one may break the circle; it has to stay tight.

After the session:

- Explain to the group how important trust is.

Trust Lean

You will need:

- No equipment required.

Site:

- Any spacious area.

How it works:

- Firstly, ensure everyone's safety by instructing group members not to fool around.
- Teach the group the spotting position: Keep your knees bent, with one foot in front of the other. Hold your arms out in front of you with your elbows at your sides, your fingers tucked together and your palms up towards the person falling.
- Divide the group into pairs. Let one partner stand in front of the other, with their back towards the other.
- The person standing at the back must now take the spotting position.
- The person standing in front must now fall back into their partner's arms. While falling back, they must keep their body stiff, with their knees straight and their arms crossed over their chest. They must simply "lean" back into the person standing behind them.
- With each fall, the person in the spotting position must let their partner fall a little further backwards, but only as far as their partner is comfortable with.
- Always make sure that group members won't hurt themselves while falling.

After the session:

- Explain the meaning and importance of trust.

Trust Run (Guillotine)

You will need:

- No equipment required.

Site:

- Outdoor area with ample space to run in.

How it works:

- Divide the group into two equal lines opposite each other. The two lines must be about one big step apart.
- The two lines must face each other, with their arms held out in front of them at shoulder height, forming a "zip".
- One person at the end of the two rows must now walk about 20 m away from the rest of the group, then run through the group's arms at full speed.
- As the runner approaches, the rest of the group must either lift or lower their hands so as not to touch the runner. If the runner flinches or ducks, they have to do it again. If they make it through without flinching, they can fall in at the other end of the row, and the next person in line becomes the runner.

Special rules:

- The group members have to stay focused all the time.

After the session:

- Ask the group whether they found the activity scary.
- Explain the importance of trust.

Trust Fall

You will need:
- 1 sturdy bench
- 1 blindfold (optional)

Site:
- Any area where it would be safe to do the activity.

How it works:
- One person is blindfolded (optional) and then has to stand on the bench with their back to the rest of the group.
- The rest of the group forms two rows opposite each other next to the bench.

- Each person must cross their arms and hold hands with the person opposite them.
- The person on the bench asks the group, "Ready?"
- The group answers, "Ready."
- The person on the bench says, "Jumping."
- The group replies, "Jump on."
- The person on the bench then has to fall back, with straight knees, their arms crossed over their chest and their feet together, into the waiting group's arms.
- The group then catches the falling person.
- After falling, the person gets in line with the rest of the group, and the next person in line gets onto the bench.

Special rules:
- The group members have to stay focused all the time.
- Warn group members that the force of catching the person will pull them forward, so they must be careful not to bump heads with the person across from them.
- A person's bum area is the heaviest part of their body, so position the stronger group members to catch that area.

After the session:
- Explain the importance of trust.
- Check the bench for any damage and put it away.
- Any damage to the bench must be reported.

Trust Walk

You will need:

- A sturdy A-frame with well-fastened ropes (see image)
- 1 blindfold (optional)

Site:

- Flat outdoor area with plenty of space.

How it works:

- One person is blindfolded (optional) and must then stand on the A-frame, holding onto the two legs of the frame.
- The other group members then have to grab hold of the ropes attached to the A-frame.
- The group's aim is to make the A-frame "walk" for 4 m with the person on it. They must use the ropes to keep the A-frame upright and manoeuvre it so that it takes "steps".

Special rules:

- The group members have to stay focused all the time.

After the session:

- Explain the importance of trust.
- Check the A-frame for any damage and put it away.
- Any damage to the A-frame must be reported.

Respectful
Guidance
Compassion
Courage
Inspire
Confidence
CHARACTER
Formative

LEADERSHIP

Diverse
Committed
Delegates
Imaginative
Hope
Attitude Social
Empathetic
Faithful
Listens
Follow through
Flexible
Responsibly
Effective
Approachable
Patience
Communicate
Creative
LOVE
Open hearted
Positive
Caring

The workshop in this section will help a group understand the basics of leadership – what a leader is and how a leader should behave.

Leadership Workshop

This workshop is divided into three activities:
- Discussion: Leadership
- Discussion: Types of leaders
- SWOT analysis

You will need:
- 1 table per group
- Paper and pencils for each group
- 1 laminated SWOT analysis sheet per person (see below)

Site:
- Anywhere comfortable.

How it works:
- Divide the group into smaller groups and let each group sit at a table.
- Give each group paper and pencils.

Discussion: Leadership

- Ask the following questions and give the groups time to discuss and write down their answers:

    1. What is a group?
       Suggested answer: A group is a number of different people (three or more) that have to achieve one goal together.

    2. What should a group do, i.e. what is the purpose of a group?
       Suggested answer: Support one another, listen to one another, respect one another, and know one another.

    3. What is a leader?
       Suggested answer: A leader is someone who can take control of a situation and who actively participates in solving problems.

4. What qualities should a leader have?
    Suggested answer: A leader should respect themselves and others, be responsible, be sympathetic to others, and have good time management, decision-making, communication and listening skills.

5. What specific duties do leaders have at your school or workplace?
    Suggested answer: Maintain order, make sure employees/pupils are happy, etc.

- The above answers are not necessarily the only correct answers but merely serve as guidelines to get the conversation going.
- Discuss the following statement with the groups: Leadership is an action, not a position.

Discussion: Types of Leaders

- There are many types of leaders, but only four will be discussed.
- You can ask group members to give more examples of types of leaders.
- Discuss each leadership style and ask the group members to think about what type of leader they are.
- Discuss the pros and cons of each leadership style.

1. Free leader (*Laissez-faire*): This type of leader allows their followers to make their own decisions. While still providing rules, the free leader does not tell their followers what to do, but only corrects them when they are out of bounds. Free leaders are usually loved by their followers, but consistency is a problem in their leadership.

2. Autocratic leader: This type of leader tells their followers what they want done and how they want it to be accomplished, without taking the advice and opinions of their followers into account.

3. Democratic leader: This type of leader includes their followers in the decision-making process.

4. Charismatic leader: This type of leader uses their personal charm to get things done.

SWOT Analysis

- This activity will give group members the opportunity to get to know themselves better.
- Give each person a SWOT analysis sheet (see the example following these instructions) and give them time to complete it themselves.
- SWOT stands for Strengths, Weaknesses, Opportunities and Threats.
- The SWOT analysis sheet provides space for group members to list items for each of the above aspects.
- Examples include:
    - Strength: Good listener
    - Weakness: Unfocused
    - Opportunity: To become a better leader
    - Threat: Stress
- Once everyone has completed their SWOT analysis, ask the group to share some of their strong points, and to point out the strong points of other group members.
- Explain that it is important to know yourself and your group members in order to be a good leader.
- Ask each group member what they think their role in the group is, e.g. an organiser, leader or follower.
- Explain to the group that before starting a task you need a plan, organisation and a strong leader.

Taking a break between sessions:
- Instruct the group members to go outside and look at something as if it is the first time they have seen it.
- Let group members stand up and use their body language to show how they feel.

After the session:
- Take in all the papers, pencils, laminated sheets, etc. and put them away.
- Put scrap paper in a recycling bin, if available.

Printable Activity Sheet

SWOT Analysis

STRENGTHS (Good listener)

WEAKNESSES (Unfocused)

OPPORTUNITIES (To become a better leader)

THREATS (Stress)

www.ingramcontent.com/pod-product-compliance
Lightning Source LLC
Chambersburg PA
CBHW040100160426
43193CB00002B/27